## Praise for
### *It's Not Because I'm Better Than You*

Don Carey's reputation as a leading NFL tackler places him in an elite category. However, the enthusiasm he has for the game and life is truly remarkable. His passion for football, youth, and the community is unmatched in the NFL today. He is a true leader of men. His book is a genuine difference maker and a definite must-read. **Joe Marciano, Special Teams Coordinator, Detroit Lions, NFL**

A motivational and inspirational read that provides a blueprint for a triumphant life despite the odds. **Jim Caldwell, Head Coach, Detroit Lions, NFL**

The power of Don's honest and practical approach to tough situations both in his life and on the field can only help others find the courage to take action in their own lives.

This book is for anyone who wants to be better at what they do. **Dr. Dana Sinclair, Ph.D., Performance Psychologist in the NFL, MLB, NBA, and NHL**

I have had the amazing pleasure of working with Don Carey since 2012, when he answered my call to athletes for support of our national youth literacy initiatives. Through our partnership with Don, we have successfully leveraged the support of corporations such as Tata Technologies, Ford Motor Company, Marathon Petroleum and others to benefit the youth of Detroit, MI. It has been a great honor to work alongside Don to benefit thousands of youth throughout the years.

"It's Not Because I'm Better Than You" is a must have and a must read! We are looking forward to having Don host reading sessions across the country with the students that we serve and gifting copies of his book to them. Job well done Don! Proud of you! **Cathleen C. Laporte, Founder & President, Athletes for Charity**

# It's Not Because I'm Better Than You

## Don J. Carey III

Published by Waldorf Publishing
2140 Hall Johnson Road
#102-345
Grapevine, Texas 76051
www.WaldorfPublishing.com

It's Not Because I'm Better Than You

ISBN: 978-1-68419-251-9
Library of Congress Control Number: 2016957059

# Table of Contents

# Dedication

To my wife, Lakeisha: You are the love of my life and my best friend. It is said that behind every strong man is an equally strong or stronger woman. You bring this statement to a whole new meaning. If God hadn't blessed me with you, I am fully confident that I would only be a shell of the man I am today. Thank you for being my constant cheerleader. Thank you for being the spine in my back that holds me up and keeps me straight. Thank you for lending an ear when I need to vent and a shoulder when I need to cry. Most of all thank you for allowing me to be the man of our house and making mc fccl like a king every time I step into the door. I love you!

To my son, Victor: You are my Pride and Joy. You arc my daily motivation. I pray that the examples I set forth are those that teach you how to be a man rightly. I pray that when you see or think of me that you are proud to call me your father. I didn't have a father during my early years of life. I pray you will never know that feeling of neglect and abandonment. I am so blessed to have you in my life. Every time I step into the door, no matter how pleasant or distressed my day is going, you greet me with the same loving smile and excitement, and it is at that moment that life is placed in its proper perspective. I love you son.

To the millions of young people who have a drive to succeed but do not know a practical way of getting to that point: My hope is that this book will help you to bridge that gap between desire and accomplishment. Pull from these pages whatever is needed to help you become the person you know you can be. I know I do not know you and probably will never meet you, but it is my love for you that drove me to write such a book as this.

## Foreword by Dr. Galen Duncan, Ph.D
## Senior Director of Player Development

I have had the unique experience of working with athletes from the NFL, NBA, College and High School Sports. I have never met/seen an athlete mature in a more appropriate fashion than Don Carey. As a young man, he struggled as we all do but the transformation has been steady and amazing. He is the most perfect husband, father, teammate, community leader, coworker, spiritual leader as well as my friend.

I was very excited when he brought his book idea to me. He first asked me to read some chapters. Don's writings reminded me of some of my own obstacles in life and left me desiring more of his works. When he asked me to write this "Foreword" I was forced to "humble myself" (something Don often tells those around him).

Don Carey is someone we can all be proud of and aspire to be like. He is approachable in an unapproachable world. He is calm and intentional in a world that is hectic and sporadic. He strives to make others great and gets his own satisfaction from emptying his giving heart. If you are reading this "Foreword," please keep reading the book. There is a message here for all, and "It's Not Because He Is Better Than You"… It's because he genuinely wants the best for you. Thank you, DC. I am truly honored.

# Introduction

When I sit back and look at my life, I'm always amazed at the things I've been able to accomplish at such a young age. Before the age of thirty, I am a College Graduate, an NFL draft pick, a CEO of my real estate company, the founder of a ministry, a co-founder of the S. T. E. M. literacy program in Detroit, a graduate student, a husband, and a proud father.

I know from the outside looking in, many may think I've been able to do all this because of talent and on some level I would agree; however, the vast majority of my accomplishments has nothing to do with my physical ability. There are far many more factors that come into play here, and this book seeks to expound on some of them. Together we will go on a journey of my life and the lessons I've learned along the way.

We will point out some key individuals who have left a lasting impact on me, as well as examine a few situations that I believe were pivotal in molding me into the man I am today. I am genuinely excited for you to take this trip down memory lane with me. I honestly believe that there are nuggets that can help you along your way. None are more important than the realization that if I can make it, so can you.

So why would I choose a title such as this? Well, I chose this title because right off the bat I wanted everyone to know that even though some people in this world are amazingly talented, I, for the most part, am not one of those individuals. I've never been the smartest person in the room. I've never been the strongest or fastest player on a team. And countless people possess far more savvy and wisdom than myself. I wanted this title to be one that causes the readers to evaluate themselves to see if they are indeed making the right decisions in life and in doing so giving them a shot to obtain the level of success we all want for ourselves.

My wife and I have been blessed to speak to so many of our youth across the nation, and I am continually shocked at the lack of a practical plan our young people have for obtaining whatever level of success they want. Sure, they know conceptually that they have to work hard, get good grades, and so on. That part has been drilled in them since they were toddlers. The issue that I am seeing is when they go from conceptual to the practical, from intangible dreams to tangible goals. Many don't have a plan. I hope and pray that this book can be a tool used by our youth to help them move along in life. As I always say, "Our children are our future. If we impact our children, especially now, we will change our future."

I want to take a little time to express what this book is not. This book is not a self-help guide to prosperity. The chapters that follow aren't promises by any means and I fully recognize that there are individuals all around the world who are the hardest working, most dedicated people around; yet they never seem to catch a break in life. I don't want to discredit them or brush their efforts aside. I fully acknowledge that apart from the grace of God on me, my efforts would ultimately result in nothing.

That's not to say that one necessarily needs to believe in God to be successful. Even though my heart's burning desire is for everyone to come to have faith in the Lord Jesus Christ, it is evident that many people who aren't Christians are either as successful or more successful than believers. Furthermore Matthew 5:45 teaches that God reigns over the just and unjust alike, meaning he will bless whom he wants. So, let's let God be God in that respect. With that being said, I believe that God has set in place many general principles that if implemented properly can increase one's chances of being successful.

So, what is a principle? For those who may not know, a principle is a fundamental truth or proposition that serves as the foundation for a system of belief or behavior or a chain of reasoning. In other words, a principle is a system of actions that if followed, generally will lead you to an anticipated outcome.

How are principles different from promises? Well, a promise is a declaration or an assurance that if someone does one thing, a particular outcome will happen. Whereas a principle acknowledges the reality that even if you follow a particular system, there is a chance the outcome, though unlikely, will not be as favorable as you hoped.

Why are principles important? Throughout the history of the world, there have been many successful individuals from all walks of life. From studying the way these people carried themselves, in most cases, we can see a pattern of actions shared amongst them. These patterns can then be systematized to form a general roadmap for others to follow, i.e., a principle. Following the example of our predecessors today is critical for us for several reasons.

Firstly, from them, we can glean key insights into what they did, how they were able to do it, and why they did what they did. There is no reason to reinvent the wheel. As the adage goes, "There is nothing new under the sun." Therefore, we can be confident that someone in the past has done what we are trying to do and learn from that person or persons. Secondly, we can see the pitfalls and mistakes that they made and hopefully learn from them. Any fool can learn from his mistakes, but a wise man learns from the mistakes of others.

Throughout the book, I will mention key individuals and stories that have impacted my life. Out of respect for these people and their privacy, I have decided to omit the names of some of them because not all of them have had a positive influence on me and that's not to say that they are bad people. I don't want to be the reason someone else has a negative view of them. You will also find places where I have inserted motivational words from players who have had an impact on me throughout my career. Some of them I'm sure you will recognize and others you may not. But know that every one of these individuals is a great strong-minded man, and if you ever get the chance to come across them, rather they are speaking or doing an appearance, make sure you are there. Their words of wisdom have the power to change lives. Trust me; I know because my life is one of them.

At the end of each chapter you find a space for you to take notes. I want to help you get the most out of this book. So please use these sections to reflect on the previous chapter, and write down any thoughts or ideas of how to apply what you've read to your life. You will also find a short message to help guide you through this process. Be as detailed as you need to be. If you need more space, I suggest you continue to write notes in a separate journal. Be sure to date each entry.

Finally, you will also see various quotes from prominent individuals scattered throughout the book. I am truly indebted to my head coach Jim Caldwell for providing a good portion of them.

Coach Caldwell has a unique ability to lead and encourage men in one of the most testosterone-driven professions in the world. He is able to do this and still maintain a clear, level-headed and logical approach to coaching that is rarely seen in today's world. Over the past three years, I have learned more from him than all my previous years in the NFL combined! I hope that as you read the pages that follow, that I am able to inspire you to think clearly, logically, and purposely about your future just as he inspired me. With that being said, let's get into the book!

## Humble Beginnings

I was born in Grand Rapids, Michigan in the late 80s to two teenage parents. My mother (Karen) was known throughout the city for her beautiful singing voice. She would always be in church leading the choir or singing a sermonic solo. I still remember us traveling all around the state going from church to church, convention to convention listening to my mom sing.

I even remember her recording her own video covering Whitney Houston's song "I Will Always Love You." My sisters and I used to sneak into her room and watch the VHS over and over. I often wonder if I hadn't come along when I did if she would have made it big like her childhood friends The Debarges, The Clarks, and Marvin Sapp did.

My father (Don, Jr.) was also a talented young man in his own right. Even though he wasn't as widely known as my mother, my dad had some serious skills on the basketball court and he also was a genius in the kitchen. One of the fondest memories that I have with him is when we made spaghetti and meatballs together. I remember trying my best to eat a whole meatball because I wanted to show him how big of a boy I was, but almost made myself throw up.

Sadly, I only have a few more fond memories with my father. Before I turned five years old, my dad was snatched away from me and my three sisters, leaving us to be raised by a single undereducated mother. Now I say 'snatched' because I truly believe that my father loved us with his whole heart and would never walk away from us if he was in the right state of mind. But when drugs came into the picture, the man who I used to know as father became a shell of his former self and with his mind blinded by the drugs that clouded his judgment, he abandoned us.

The worst part was that he didn't go far. My dad lived less than one mile from us with another woman. Right down the street from the elementary school I attended. To make matters even worse, the lady who babysat us stayed a few houses down from my dad, yet he would rarely see us and the few times he did see us we didn't want to be around him because of the lifestyle he lived. I remember feeling so hurt when he left that I would often write poems about dying because I felt so worthless. I would constantly ask myself what was wrong with me that my daddy didn't want me?

I didn't understand the power that drugs can have on a man. That confusion would soon turn into anger, and that anger would then turn into hate. I hated my father for not being there for us. I hated him for forcing my mom to work two jobs and still barely have enough to take care of us. I hated him for every tear that I shed on nearly a nightly basis. I hated him that I had to learn what a real man looked like from my next-door neighbor. I hated my father for every man I turned to looking for someone to fill the void he left in my life, only to be disappointed time and time again. To those readers who are fathers, please never forget to be present in the life of your children.

The greatest influence anyone can have on the youth is not money or gifts, but time. I am always amazed at how my son, even at such a young age, looks to me to learn what and what not to do. From time to time I catch him staring at me mimicking whatever I am doing at the moment. In his inquisitive eyes, I am the standard of manhood. The image of what he should and should not do. And as such I could never neglect him the way my father ignored me as a young man. Please never allow your children to ask "What is wrong with me that my daddy didn't want me?"

I want to pause here and make something very clear. I didn't include the above information about my dad because I want you to have a negative view of him or to try and take shots at him for not being there for our family. I love my father with all my heart, and the Lord knows my heart yearns to see him delivered from his addictions so we can once again have a relationship together.

I do however want to make a point. I don't know when my father began smoking weed. I do, however, know that weed was the catalyst that fed my father's drug addiction, eventually leading him down the road to cocaine. So, when people, including myself, say weed is a gateway drug, that's not a mantra to me. I've lived that pain. I've cried myself to sleep because I felt as if my daddy didn't love me. I know many people ask what's wrong with smoking weed? I'm still waiting for someone to tell me what's right about it…

We grew up on the southeast side of Grand Rapids. I won't sit here and paint a picture making my neighborhood seem worse than what it was. Nevertheless, I will say it had its moments. Just like most inner-city areas we had a few knuckleheads who wanted to be gangbangers and others who wanted to sell drugs. But for the most part, it was a typical lower-middle class neighborhood, with most families working hard to provide a stable life.

There is an adage that says when you are poor you don't know it because the riches of love and togetherness outweigh the material things. I agree and disagree with that saying. I agree because even though we didn't have much, we always had each other. That bond continues to this day. Not a day goes by that I don't speak to at least two of my six siblings. The part that I disagree with is "you don't know it." Even though we were rich in love and togetherness, it was plain to see we struggled in other areas.

I remember having nightmares at night and going to lay at my mom's door. I could often hear her cry as she sat on her bed. She later told me that she was used to deciding between feeding her children or paying bills and would sit on her bed crying to the Lord to send some relief. My sister

(Vickia), who is six years older than myself, knew the situation that we were in and would often wear boys' clothes and pass them down to me when I could fit into them.

I thank God for groups like TLC who made her life a little easier so that she didn't have to explain why she did what she did. Other than that, the only time I would get "new" clothes was when my older cousins would give me their old clothes. But even in the midst of our poverty I thoroughly enjoyed my childhood. Till this day I remember my neighbors and playing football in the front yard or playing basketball in the alleyway.

This was my life until my first year in high school. I used to play running back on the freshman football team at Central High. One day after a scrimmage my mom came up to me with this guy at her side. His name was William Robinson, but everyone called him Rob. Right away Rob began giving me coaching points on my game. In the back of my mind, I'm like who is this guy? Next thing I know my mom is telling us we were moving down to Norfolk, Virginia to live with Rob. Even though I hated leaving Grand Rapids, the time I've spent with Rob has had a profound impact on the man I am today. We will revisit the rest of this story later in chapter seven.

I wanted to give you a little bit of my background upfront to show you that I wasn't born with a silver spoon in my mouth. Not that there is anything wrong with someone being born into a wealthy family. I, however, was not one of those blessed individuals. Furthermore, I know that the vast majority of people who will read this book were either born into a similar situation or worst situations than myself. I want you to know that it's not where you begin but where you go from there.

Even though my upbringing was rough, I never let that dictate what I wanted to do in life and where I wanted to go. Charles Swindle once said, "We are all faced with a series of great opportunities brilliantly disguised as impossible situations." None of us can control the families that we are born into. No one can choose the social or economic status of his family. We can, however, decide to let our situation motivate or destroy us. We can opt to carry on the same old status quo or be the one who breaks the link in the chain of mental bondage that plagues so many in our community.

I made up my mind that I would never follow in the footsteps of those whose actions would lead them down a path of destruction. Rather I would be one of the ones carving new steps for myself and anyone audacious enough to follow me. If you have not already made this decision for yourself, I suggest you do so sooner than later. I hope the pages that follow will aid in the continuation of that declaration or provide the spark that inspires its genesis.

Take time to reflect on your life and your experiences. Regardless of if they have been good or bad, write them down and use those experiences as motivation moving forward.

_____

_____

_____

_____

_____

_____

_____

_____

_____

_____

_____

_____

_____

_____

# Derek Cox

## Response-Ability

Life is all about how we respond to adversity. We will face situations and circumstances that we feel we don't deserve. We will go through struggles, trials, and conflict. We will be good people and have bad things happen to us. We will see good things happen to bad people, but simply stated: "Life is not fair." However, our ability to respond positively is fair. We have been created with a wonderful response-ability to choose a positive response over a negative one. So, let's take our response-ability and determine we will overcome adversity with positivity. Success in all areas of life (i.e. family, friends, career, school, etc.) is a matter of responding appropriately to adversity, and we all have the response-ability to do it positively.

# John Wendling

I've always been a man of few words. Humility, a grateful attitude, and relentless hard work are keys to live by. Failures are inevitable as we go through life. Count them as a blessing, and use them as an opportunity to learn and grow. Each day will be different posing its unique joys and challenges. Your attitude in approaching it is everything and your reactions along the way guide and shape your future. How do you know when you are as great as you'll ever be? When you decide to quit learning. Remember to stay humble through life's successes, and ready to grow through life's tribulations.

## The Deception of Talent

Several years ago, I went back to my alma mater Norfolk State University to catch up with my old defensive back coach. As I walked into his office, there was a player sitting at his desk watching a film. My coach goes on to tell me all about this guy and how he really had a chance to make it to the NFL, just like I did. With great enthusiasm, I begin telling the young man everything that I had to do in order to give myself a shot at the league. To my dismay, the young man seemed to brush off everything I was telling him and continued to watch the film. I turned to see what he was watching, and I immediately see him making play after play on the field.

I quickly put two and two together. In his mind, everything that I was telling him was either partially or completely irrelevant because clearly he was "Ball'n". I have to admit I was a bit thrown off by his response. When I was in his shoes, I would have loved for someone to give me a roadmap or an idea of the type of work I would have to put in to make it. But clearly this young man thought his situation was different from mine. I admit the guy was a monster on the field. And from the short time I watched him he was a man amongst boys. He was truly talented. Nevertheless, things didn't go as planned for him; he didn't get drafted.

There was one thing the young man failed to realize. Even though he had talent, he had even more talent than the guys he was playing against. How did his talent measure up to the thousands of players he didn't play against? Yes, talent is important, but I've learned that with each level of competition (i.e. high school, college, and pros), the talent disparity evens out. By this I mean a player who is leaps and bounds above everyone else on the high school level, may be an average player at the collegiate level. And a great collegiate player may not even show up on the radar of a professional team. With each level of competition, players tend to start looking more and more alike from a talent standpoint.

## A Blessing and A Curse

The above story is not at all an isolated incident. We all know someone who fits this mold or a similar one. I believe that talent is both a blessing and a curse when it comes to the majority of people. It is a blessing because it gives one the potential to succeed in whatever avenue they are in; however, it can be a curse because it tends to blind some from reality. Here are a few examples. You may be a talented defensive back in college, a true shutdown corner. In reality, your backpedal is horrible, you are just quicker than everyone else which allows you to make up the slack.

Or you may be a talented wide receiver, touted as the next Calvin Johnson. But in reality, your routes are in need of help, but your hand-eye coordination is off the charts. I could go on and on, and this same logic can be applied to other areas of life as well. But the point I'm trying to make is what would happen with that defensive back, or that wide receiver if he comes across another player with equal or greater talent? Will that player then be able to rely on their God-given talent? Maybe, but in my experience, people who take this approach fail more times than not.

No matter what career path you plan to follow in life, there has to be something that separates you from the rest of the pack. Simply relying on your talent level, in most cases, won't get it done for you. As I mentioned before, there is a select group of individuals who own that innate ability which allows them to stick out no matter what. But even if there was a chance that I were that person, I would still want to do more to distinguish myself. Simply because I don't know what the person in the next state over is doing. Or what talent level he or she has. Let's not be deceived; for the vast majority of us, there is always somebody out there who looks just like you and possibly even better. Yes, every person is unique in their own way, but at the end of the day, there are only so many ways to do the same job. A backpedal will always be a back pedal no matter the person doing it. This was never more true to me than the first time I was cut by an NFL team in 2011.

## A Lesson in Humility

I had just come off my first season as the starting free safety for the Jacksonville Jaguars. Up until that point, I had given everything I had in preparation for this position I found myself in. But for whatever reason, be it cockiness or immaturity, I began to feed into the mantra of talent that was being shrouded around my name. In layman's terms, I was feeling myself. During camp, I compared myself to the other safeties on the team and thought that the talent and versatility I brought would assure me a roster spot. I became comfortable and I did not prepare the same way I was used to, and as a result, my plays suffered.

As camp came to an end, I found myself barely playing in preseason games and some games I didn't play at all, yet the reality of what was about to happen still didn't sink in. On the last day of roster cuts, I surprisingly received that dreaded phone call from the front office telling me to bring in my playbook. I was so confused. I felt that I was better than the other safeties on the roster, and that there wasn't another defensive back on the team who could play all the positions the way I did.

After meeting with the coaches and front office personnel, I was escorted out of the building. As I was walking out, I looked up and saw another defensive back, being escorted by a ProScout, walking right towards me. And it was at that moment I realized the error of my ways. Yes, I was one of the most talented players on the current Jacksonville roster, but I never factored in the myriads of other players around the country, both on the collegiate level and in the NFL, grinding hard every day and sacrificing whatever was necessary to take this spot... my spot. It is one thing to have someone beat you out of a roster spot, this will happen from time to time. But it's another thing to blatantly give it away, which is exactly what I did.

As a result, I spent the next several months on the couch not receiving so much as a phone call from other teams. To make matters worse, I was not financially responsible with my money, and before I was released, I lived that baller life we all see on television. I partied like a rock star. Club hopped all around Miami south beach. I bought what I wanted when I wanted it. And I lived as if I was a millionaire, but in reality, I was only a thousandaire. I quickly found myself looking at an empty account just days before bills were due. I had to start turning off utilities because I feared I wouldn't be able to pay them.

It is only by the grace of God that I was picked up by the Detroit Lions several months later due to injury, but honestly, who wants to be at the mercy of someone else's misfortunes? Nevertheless, had I focused on improving my craft and using that in conjunction with my God-given talents, instead of leaning wholly on talent, I truly believe that I would have had a much different experience my first couple of years in the NFL. I quickly went from a young player with tons of potential to being another notch in the statistical failure category.

The vast majority of players who were in a similar situation as I, quickly find themselves out of the NFL wishing they could have done this differently or that differently. They now understand the true weight of the saying, "The NFL means Not For Long". Though it takes many years to make it to this level, it can be snatched away in an instant. This is a key principle in life.

The opportunity of a lifetime only exists within the lifetime of that opportunity, and we must be prepared for our *Kairos*, appointed time, moments. In order for us to *carpe diem*, make the most out of these moments, our preparation has to consist of continually refining our skills and knowledge of our career field, so that they may compliment the talents we have and carve a space for us to succeed in life. There is no dichotomy between talent and hard work. Rather the two go hand in hand. Thomas Edison once said, "Opportunity is missed by most people because it is dressed in overalls and looks like work."

My hope for you is that you won't fall into the same trap that I and countless others have fallen into. There is an old adage which says that any fool can learn from his own mistakes, but a wise man learns from the mistakes of others. Don't just look at my faults and brush them off as me being an idiot; even though that's exactly what I was, and go about your day as if you could never find yourself in my shoes. The deceptive thing about deception is that those being deceived don't realize it until it's too late.

And if history has shown us nothing else, it has shown us billions of regretful people wishing they would've heeded the words of wisdom passed down to them. Let my stumbling block be the building block that reminds you of the fragility of success and the importance of honoring every moment, treating it with the respect and attention it deserves. That respect must begin by accompanying our God given talents with the necessary work ethic to get us a shot at the outcome we are seeking.

As a special teams ace, every Sunday I line up against two of the best special teams players on the opposing team. More times than not these two individuals are more talented, faster, and younger than I am. Yet, time and time again I win more than I lose. Throughout my career, I've been able to improve every year despite me getting older and less athletic. Why? Because I have trained myself to be able to operate at a critically efficient level that most people never reach. And most people will never reach this level simply because of their perception of success, in my profession and many others, is totally wrong.

I am amazed at how when I meet a stranger, and they find out I play in the NFL, often the first thing they say is, "you're too small to be an NFL player." I laugh to myself because in their eyes, the only ones who are supposed to do what I do are the six-foot three inch first round draft picks or the poster boy quarterback we see in the television commercials. Even though the NFL has its share of Goliath and Hercules-type men, the average player looks just like you and me. And after meeting so many people who have the same mindset as the stranger above, I've come to the point that I truly believe most people have absolutely no idea what it takes to rise to the top of their field.

I believe this has far more to do with their glorification of talent over emphasizing the realization of hard work and the cultural acceptance of mediocrity as a personality trait. By this I mean, if the NFL is only reserved for those who are genetically gifted and more talented than others, then there is no reason for those of us who aren't as genetically gifted or as talented to even try. If this is true, we can settle for never reaching our potential. If this is true, we can settle for our dreams never becoming a reality. If this is true, there is no hope for the vast majority of people on the Earth.

But thank God this is not true. We CAN reach our potential. We CAN make our dreams reality. There IS hope for us to succeed in life. But that hope has to come on the backs of those who are willing to prepare for it. Even though talent is important, it is only the studs in the house of success. The foundation, however, is found in the preparation we put into it.

List the thing(s) that you are truly passionate about. Instead of relying wholly on talent to be successful in that area, what are some things that you can do to help separate yourself from the rest of the pack?

_____

_____

_____

_____

_____

_____

_____

_____

_____

_____

_____

_____

_____

# Haloti Ngata

Good is the worst enemy of the best.

Throughout my life, I was always told that I was good. And it was being good at anything I was doing. Sports, school, scouts, faith, being a son or brother, etc. As I got used to being good at everything, I realized I wasn't going to be able to grow because I settled for good. I was never going to be great or the best because I settled. So, my advice to you is: start being good and you can be good at whatever you want to be. But don't stay there and be satisfied. Continue to grow and be the best. Remember good is the worst enemy of the best.

# Jason Hanson

I've heard it said, 'Pursue excellence instead of success'. That has been one of my favorite insights and something I have always tried to do with any endeavor. I've seen that you can be successful without being excellent: you can win by being lucky, by cheating, or by cutting corners. While those wins may get the title of 'success', they are usually superficial, fragile, and temporary victories. They say nothing worthwhile about who you are. Excellence is a far greater quality. First, striving for excellence is something that involves becoming the best you can be and develops character, and that is something that has value in every aspect of life. And second, your best chance of success actually comes from being excellent! And that success is built to last. Pursue excellence instead of success.

## Critical Efficiency

One of my most favorite years in the NFL was 2014. That year was full of so many exciting twists and turns. From unexpected injuries to nail-biting finishes. From a record setting year for Calvin Johnson to me taking a fumble recovery forty plus yards for my first touchdown. Amongst those moments, one of my favorites came when we played the New Orleans Saints at Ford Field in Detroit, Michigan. New Orleans jumped on us early and held a 23-17 lead late in the fourth quarter.

Although the game was pretty evenly matched, the scoreboard, for the most part, did not reflect that. On the second to last drive, I remember vividly Glover Quinn stepping in front of a Drew Brees pass and intercepting it, nearly returning it for a touchdown with three minutes left in the game. Quarterback Matthew Stafford would soon after connect with wide receiver Corey Fuller on a pass in the back of the end zone for the game-winning touchdown.

If Glover hadn't made that play, I doubt very seriously, that we would have won that day. From the outside looking in people think Glover made a great play at a crucial moment, which he absolutely did! But what many didn't know or failed to realize is that opportunity didn't come because he was only a talented player, which he is. It came from the countless hours of hard work he put in leading up to that very moment.

Eliud Kipchoge once said, "A champion is not made in a moment of victory, but in the seconds, hours, days, weeks, and months of preparation." Because of the work he put in throughout the week, Glover was able to recognize the formation, understand situational football and what the Saints wanted to do. Which would then put him in the perfect position for his skill set to shine.

From the very first day that I met Glover he has been the same person. He has always focused on the details meticulously regardless of the situation, be it a walk through, practice or a game. And it is this approach to his craft that has allowed him to exemplify a trait known as Critical Efficiency. This trait is best described as the ability to perform at the highest level, under pressure, in hostile environments, and in the most critical situations. Watching Glover these past years reminds me of an old proverb that says, "If you see a man who is diligent in his ways. That man will stand amongst kings, and not mere people."

I've seen this principle play out in the lives of so many NFL players like Glover. To be diligent is to show a consistent and intentional effort towards one job or work as well as having a painstaking awareness of the most minute details. But that level of diligence is harder for most people to sustain. I believe this is largely due to the fact that most of us don't realize there is an extreme level of commitment of time and energy that is required to not only reach a certain point but to also remain there. I often joke with people that I've played football since I was five years old and it has been the longest relationship I've ever had.

But if we really examine my life, I am a good football player because I've put a constant commitment of time and energy into this area and have done so for over an extended period of time. Thus, the success I've had is really to be expected because of the work I've put in. Now there is a little more to it than what I just said, and we will cover that later in this chapter. But the point I'm trying to make here is no matter what you want to do in your life, it will require an extreme commitment of time and energy to rise to the top of that field. There is no other way. General Colin Powell once said, "There are no secrets to success: Don't waste time looking for them."

## So how much time and energy are we talking?

Well, according to Malcolm Gladwell's book "*Outliers*", it takes about ten thousand hours of training in a field to become an expert. That may seem extreme or nonsensical to you, but I assure you that it is not only legit but also conservative.

After the 2012 Olympics, the National Lottery completed a poll in which they found that Olympic athletes spent around ten thousand hours preparing for one event. That means if you would have added the amount of time spent in training sessions, the average Olympian spent one year, one month, and twenty days preparing for a shot at performing on one of the world's largest stages. Notice that they were training for a shot at the Olympics. They had not yet qualified.

They did this because they understand the old Navy Seal lore that "under pressure you don't rise to the occasion, rather you sink to the level of your training." These modern-day gladiators can stay focused for so long because to them their event is much more than just a hundred-meter dash or long jump. These people have a deep intimate connection with these events because they know that they are doing what they are uniquely gifted to do.

To them, it is much more than a job or work. It's closer to a calling or a vocation, which is a strong feeling or suitability for a particular career. If you do not have this same passion about what you want to do, and this same drive pushing you every single day, then you will not prepare adequately enough to perform at a critically efficient level.

## How do you know if you're truly passionate about something?

This is not at all a rhetorical question, because up until my senior year at Norfolk State, I hadn't realized my deep connection with football. I had grown so accustomed to practicing, weight lifting, and running sprints and drills all year around, that I never really gave thought to live without it. I remember the first time the realization that I may never play football again crept into my mind. It was after my last collegiate game, my senior year, at Norfolk State. We had just finished beating Winston-Salem University and were heading back to the locker room to shower and go home. As I took off my shoulder pads, I felt a rush of emotion as if I had lost a loved one or a close childhood friend.

This emotion was so strong that I couldn't hold back the tears. I cried so hard and uncontrollably that I could barely move for a few minutes. I loved and still love this game. Through it, I have been able to do so much in life, go to so many places and meet so many people. Most important of all, if I hadn't played this game, I wouldn't have met the most phenomenal woman in my life… my beautiful wife. This passionate connection is not unique to me at all.

Nearly every time an athlete gives his or her speech at their Hall of Fame induction, you see them fighting to hold back the tears as they reminisce about their playing days. Or, look at a player who announces their retirement. Often they do so with tears in their eyes. For the prime example, we need to look no further than Alex Rodriguez's retirement speech. With tears in his eyes, often having to pause to gather himself, he said, "I never thought I could play 22 years. At 18 I just wanted to make the team."

The realization that he would never play the game of baseball again hit him as he thanked the team he loved and appreciated and said his goodbyes to the game. You know you are truly passionate about something when that something is taken away from you, or threatened to be taken away, and you feel a [gaping] whole in your heart or a rush of emotion. Think of your goals, your dreams, and ambitions; now imagine if those things or that thing was taken away. How would it impact you? How would you feel about it? If the answer is anything less than some sort of emotional loss or a longing, then you need to reevaluate your goals and dreams.

Dick Nogleberg once said, "If what you believe doesn't affect how you live, then it isn't very important." You know you are truly passionate about something when your life is impacted by it. You know when you design your life around that thing, rather it is the school you go to, the clothes you wear, the way you carry yourself, or the people you hang out with. You know you are passionate about something when a good portion of your finances are spent on it, and you find yourself talking about it all the time.

## How To Reach Critical Efficiency

In my short time of being a father, I have learned a great deal about the human body from watching my son. Amongst the many things he is teaching me, I've learned that we are truly creatures of habit. By this I mean, the things we do often are really the things we do well. My defensive back coach Alan Williams calls it 'being habitized'. Furthermore, the things we do often eventually are so ingrained into our subconscious that we do them without even thinking about it.

Every day before we eat dinner our family prays together. For the longest time, my son would look at his mommy and daddy with a blank stare as we said our grace. Several months ago, my wife noticed that as we sat down to pray before dinner, that my son had also put his hands together with us. Nowadays when we sit down to eat, he is ready to pray before we even say, "Let's pray Victor." In his short lifetime he had been so habitized that this is what we do before we eat, that subconsciously he knows to do it without even thinking about it. This caused me to look back on my life to see if the same principle has been evident for me as well. And surely enough it was.

During my college days, I always wondered why none of the guys I played with made it to the NFL. I felt as if we had so much talent come through Norfolk State, that at least one of those guys would get a shot. But year after year I heard the same old story from the coaches. Such and such was good enough to play at the professional level, but the scouts didn't like him. I began to look at the guys and what they were doing and noticed that the vast majority of them only ran when the team ran or lifted when the team would lift, or watched film when the team watched film. Most guys didn't do anything to separate themselves from the rest of the pack.

I remember, during the spring of my sophomore year, two of my teammates, Daniel Hammett and Andre Twine, would always do a little more than the rest, so naturally, I began to tag along with them. Nearly every day we woke up around 6:00 am to workout with the track team. Why? Because the football lifting program was geared towards being powerful whereas the track team focused more on being explosive. We'd then go to class, then come back to lift and run with the football team.

Afterward, we'd run with the track team or work on DB drills depending on the day. We did this the entire spring and summer because we noticed the need to do more to make us better. Without even knowing it, I was beginning to put more time and energy into becoming a complete football player. The first couple weeks of training this way was tough on my body. At first, I felt as if I was putting myself through hell without seeing any results. But something interesting happened around three weeks into training. It was easier to get up in the mornings. I didn't mind all the running and lifting. My body wasn't as sore anymore.

I was beginning to habitize myself in this way of life. I would go on to have my best season at Norfolk State. I led the team in interceptions and made multiple game-winning plays to help us get to the conference championship. Furthermore, it was that year that NFL scouts began to take notice of me. All because I had habitized myself properly, which allowed me to play at an efficient critical level.

When striving for critical efficiency, it is important that we take an honest look at our situations as to evaluate what needs to change, if anything. As we looked at the football team, we saw a need to be more explosive, which led us to work with the track team. We also must make sure that we are habitizing ourselves properly. By this I mean do the things necessary to improve in whatever area you are focusing on. We've all heard the saying 'practice makes perfect', of which I completely agree. But that practice must be done with intentionality and purpose.

We must never confuse work with activity. There has to be a reason you are doing what you are doing. And there has to be a way for you to measure your progress. Any other approach to work is a waste of time and energy. Throughout my career, I have dealt with several hamstring tears. One day during practice our head coach came to me and asked why I ran so hard knowing that I could easily re-injure my hamstring and miss game time. I told him if I didn't run a certain way then my angles would be off.

The only way I could properly prepare myself was to train in a way that best matched the intensity of a game so that I would be able to recognize any adjustments that would need to be made. This is the same approach we all must have. When you work in such an intense manner, it forces your body to be pushed to its limits which in turn forces you to get better than you would have gotten had you prepared in a lesser fashion. Furthermore, you will also get to that point faster than you would had you trained in a lessor fashion.

## Persistence is Crucial

Lastly, the most difficult part of habitizing ourselves is persistence. As I mentioned above, it takes about three weeks before your body becomes acclimated to doing something. Here is where most people fail. Being accustomed to doing something is not the same as doing that thing unconsciously. There is still more work to be done. From there, it will take about ninety days before a new habit is formed. Now I want to be upfront with you. This looks good on paper, but in reality this is dreadfully hard to do.

You will essentially be working to transform your way of life. Which is most likely going to require you to abandon some old habits and as the old adage goes, "Old habits die hard." Nevertheless, through persistence and stick-to-itiveness, YOU CAN DO THIS! You're going to need a lock jaw mentality, an unwavering mindset that can't easily be moved.

In his letter addressed to his younger self, Ray Allen said, "The men who you are going to win championships with are all going to be very different people. What makes them champions is the boring old habits that nobody sees. They compete to see who can be the first to get to the gym and the last to leave." Get used to doing the boring things over and over. Get used to making the sacrifices necessary to place yourself in the best situation and best environment possible to succeed. Get used to pouring long hours and sleepless nights over your craft.

Ray continues on, "But in order to achieve your dreams, you will become a different kind of person. You'll become a bit obsessive about your routine. This will come at a heavy cost to some of your friends and family. Most nights, you won't go out. Your friends will ask why. You won't drink alcohol, ever. People will look at you funny. When you get to the NBA, you won't always play cards with the boys. Some people will assume you're not being a good teammate. You'll even have to put your family on the back burner for your job." Sacrifices must be made to reach that level of critical efficiency.

The first law of thermodynamics says that energy can neither be created nor destroyed. Practically, this means we only have so much energy to work with and cannot create any more. There are only 24 hours in a day no matter how you look at it. Which means you only have so much time to allocate activities. Remember I said critical efficiency requires an extreme amount of time and energy, so you will have to change other aspects of your life. Aspects that before were okay and tolerable, but now will become distractions.

Even though they may not be directly related to whatever you are working on, these aspects of your life can have a major impact on you reaching your goals. Only you can determine what these aspects are. I pray that you are able to objectively look at yourself and see what or who needs to be removed because if they are not, they can distract you. A coach once told me, "What you do off the field carries onto the field, there is no on/off switch."

## Make Sure Your Ribs are Showing

I've been blessed to be around some great players in the NFL. None have had a greater impact on me than Rashean Mathis. I always sat right behind him in meetings both as we were playing for the Jacksonville Jaguars and the Detroit Lions. And through observation alone, he has taught me so much. I remember during a meeting coach Alan Williams asking Rashean why he took so many notes? At that time Rashean was a twelve-year veteran, but he always took notes as if it was his first time learning the defense. Rashean took notes like this because he understood that there is always a nuance and some little detail that could make him better. He was never content with what he learned the day before and was always asking questions and trying to learn something new.

After he had retired, Rashean told the defensive backs to always make sure our ribs were showing. By this, he meant never become complacent. Stay hungry for more knowledge. Stay hungry for getting better. Stay hungry for being the best at what you do. The best NFL players are those who are students of the game. This is also true for other professions as well. Those who are fully committed to knowing the ins and outs of their craft are truly the ones who excel. And really this is a common sense principle.

Would you go to a doctor for surgery if you weren't confident that they knew the human body? Or would you allow someone to manage your finances if they had no background in financial management? Of course not. Same goes for our goals. I would have never made it to the NFL had I not known football. A lawyer would have never passed the bar had they not studied for it. A police officer would have never made the force if they hadn't passed the academy. Educating yourself is the essential to accomplishing what you want in life.

Dr. Harry Edwards once told me, "Most people who follow someone down the pipeline to the trash heap of history, do so because they are intellectually lazy." Your brain is your greatest tool, the most powerful computer on Earth. Don't allow yourself to be one of those people who look back on the history of their life and regret not using it to its full potential. Many people complain that education is too expensive. My response is just to wait until they get the bill for ignorance.

That bill is full of regret, shame, wasted potential, missed opportunities, missed financial gains, failed ventures, failed relationships to name a few. Tim Grover once said, "Your power source is from the neck up and not down." Feed that source, because for the vast majority of us, our brains will be around long after our knees, hips, elbows, and shoulders give out.

Being good at what you are passionate about may come natural to you, however, performing at the highest level will require much more than talent. Write down the necessary steps you will need to take in order to perform at that critically efficient level.

_____

_____

_____

_____

_____

_____

_____

_____

_____

_____

_____

_____

_____

# Josh Wilson

My parents each taught me lessons that I live by day in and day out.

My father taught me to take every moment seriously and never find yourself unprepared because the moment that you yearn for does not wait for you to be ready. That moment, that opportunity will come when it is ready. You must live every second prepared to relish that moment, so that when it arrives you would be excited and not regretful.

My mother taught me that I am more powerful than I know. I must learn to expose that untapped power and to be bigger than I know myself to be. If you believe opinions about yourself and never reach inside, you will never be a dominant force on this earth but rather an average citizen. People are waiting for us to quit on ourselves, to not believe we can conquer any mountain put in front of us. The difference between the successful and the average is solely the ability they have to expose their true strength. When they dig inside no one will be able to stop them.

# Scott Starks

Know Thy Self!

I once had a coach who would always say, "Know thyself!" What he meant by that was, know who you are better than anyone else... know your strengths, weaknesses, talents, gifts, personality, etc. Play (the game of life) in a way that magnifies your strengths, while simultaneously not allowing your weaknesses to hold you back (no excuses). Be the best you God created you to be. You are original, so why settle for being a cheap copy attempting to mimic another man. Be comfortable being you! Know thyself...

## Dealing with Distractions

Towards the end of the football season of my senior year in high school, I began to prepare a makeshift highlight tape to send out to colleges and universities. I remember sending one to Norfolk State University thinking if I couldn't get a scholarship at a big school, I could at least land one here. Especially since I had already received an academic scholarship from the Engineering Department.

However, the response I was given from the head coach at the time nearly destroyed any hope that I had of playing at the collegiate level. He basically told me I was too small and didn't have the right skill set to play D-1 ball. Now I will admit that I was a whopping 150 pounds when I graduated from high school, but I figured that the little bit of talent I did have plus my speed would be enough to at least get a partial scholarship. If that wasn't bad enough, out of all the schools I sent my tape to very few responded, and those who did wanted me to walk on and hopefully earn a scholarship later. But I knew my family couldn't afford to do something like that.

So, because things didn't pan out the way I wanted I was ready to give up on my dream. I was ready to walk away from the game of football. I felt as if I'd failed and somehow wasn't good enough to get the job done on the next level. The rejection I received from the various schools and that coach seemed eerily similar to the rejection that I had come to know from my younger years. And honestly, that was a feeling I was no longer interested in entertaining. So, I decided to take the academic route instead of the athletic one.

Several weeks later I received a call from Norfolk State. It was from the new football coach, Pete Adrian. Apparently, the previous one had been fired. Coach Adrian went on to offer me a full scholarship and said I reminded him of a player he once coached at Bethune-Cookman named Rashean Mathis. I was so shocked that I hung up on him. He called back moments later, and I accepted his offer of course.

Now over a decade later I find myself sitting at this desk writing to you about my life as an accomplished NFL player. All because of what many saw as trash, one man saw as treasure. I went on to start all four years at Norfolk State

University and became the first football player to play in one of the three major college all-star games. I was the first to be drafted into the NFL since Kenneth McDaniel and James Roe were taken by the Dallas Cowboys and Baltimore Ravens in the 1996 NFL Draft.

I know some of you are maybe wondering what this has to do with distractions, so let me enlighten you. Because of the words of that coach coupled with the multiple rejections I received from various schools, I was ready to give up on my dream. I let the words of others and what they thought of me distract me from what I knew I could do. Aristotle once said, "Criticism is something you can easily avoid by saying nothing, doing nothing, and being nothing." By this, he meant that anyone who had the audacity to dare to do something or be someone in life would inevitably be met with people who would be critical of that actually coming true.

Furthermore, in that moment of criticism, I let my worth and value be determined by someone who knew little to nothing about me. Author and civil rights leader Audre Lorde once said, "If I didn't define myself for myself, I would be thrown into other's fantasies of me and eaten alive." By this, she meant someone will always have an opinion of you. Rather it is good or bad is not what's important. What's important is that you set the standard for you. Who you are, how you act, what you want, and how good you can be. Because if you don't people will assume. And often that assumption portrays a shell of who you really are or it portrays a completely different person altogether.

Who are you? It's the most fundamental question you will ever have to ask. And until you find that answer, the opinions of others will always be a distraction for you. There is an old African proverb that says, "When there is no enemy within, the enemies outside cannot hurt you." Solidify who you are and have faith and confidence in that person. And never let the words of people who have no idea the amount of work, commitment, and sacrifice you put into your craft deter you from your goal.

My response to rejection was quite possibly the worst way I could have handled the situation. Just because someone else doesn't believe in your dream or your goal doesn't mean you have to follow suit. And just because you fail a few times doesn't mean you need to give up. Maybe you only need to make some adjustments. Or maybe you just need to try a different approach. One of my favorite quotes comes from the legendary Michael Jordan. He said, "I've missed more than 9000 shots in my career. I've lost almost 300 games. 26 times I've been trusted to take the game-winning shot... and missed. I've failed over and over and over again in my life. That is why I succeed."

Furthermore, many people don't know Michael was cut from the basketball team when he was in high school. Yet, he attributes his success to the many failures he had in his life. Imagine what would have happened if Michael allowed his past failures and the naysayers to distract him from working towards his goal. Imagine if there was no Michael. Would there have been an Allen Iverson? Kobe Bryant? Lebron James? All of which say they wanted to play basketball because they wanted to be like Mike! Now imagine who would be impacted if you allowed distractions to steer you away from your goal.

It's easy to think that we are the only ones affected by the decisions we make. But the reality is that no matter who you are or what you will do, there is always someone who needs to meet you, see your video, listen to your lecture, read your book, or hear your life story to gain the necessary inspiration for them to succeed. None of us were born in a bubble, and none of us will grow up in one either. Like the ripples that flow from a pebble hitting a pond, every one of us, no matter how small or insignificant we may think we are, have the power to leave a lasting impact in some way on this Earth.

Never underestimate your importance in the lives of others. I believe the reason God gave us all a unique fingerprint is to show us that we all are just that... unique. And each individual is uniquely gifted to do something. Never let the words of others and social norms dictate the level of significance of your uniqueness, rather work to show them their need for someone such as yourself. This will, of course, require you to be yourself.

I never understood why some people wanted to be like another person. You only have two options in this area. You can be the real you or the fake someone else. The real you comes naturally, and it is something that no one else, no matter how great an imitator they may be, could ever come close to mimicking.

Like most people, I used to only focus on the end goal and not the process. But I've learned that looking at life this way is similar to a man who wants to cut down a forest but only focuses on the forest itself instead of dealing with the trees one by one. Every day that he wakes up, he is disappointed that he hasn't yet reached his goal. With each passing day, that frustration grows to the point that he ends up giving up on it all together. That's how many of us think. We all have a goal set for ourselves, but we are so enamored by the outcome that we forget to fall in love with the process.

Now there is nothing wrong with having your goal in mind. I am not saying that we should work blindly. I am a firm believer that we must always work with an intent of reaching a particular outcome. I am, however, saying when we place too much focus and/or when we place our primary focus on that end goal instead of the process, the very thing we desire most can itself become a distraction. Conversely, when we put our focus on the process of reaching an end goal, we will have a different outlook on life. Through trial and error, we will learn that each process is as fluid as liquid water, constantly changing and adapting to fit its current situation. Those moments when it is time for the process to change will often be marked by failure.

Like pain in the body, failure is the alarm that lets us know it is time to adjust or fix something. When your body is hurting, no one seeks to just cut off the ailing body part, rather you find ways to fix the issues so that the pain stops and the body continues to function properly. We should take the same approach to perfecting our process. I can't stress enough the importance of what I just said. I've seen this play out negatively so many times while at Norfolk State.

Every spring, around March, NFL scouts would come to Norfolk State to run drills and tests with the seniors in what's called a "Pro Day." Typically, scouts only come to look at a handful of guys, but they will allow every senior to participate in most of the drills. Year after year I see guys eagerly chasing after their dream to play in the NFL only to be met with the sobering reality that they are utterly unprepared to capture the moment.

One year as some of the players met with scouts I remember being shocked that one of my teammates was going to participate. He was a guy who walked onto the team maybe a year earlier and never played unless it was late in the game and the team was winning big. I could tell from his body that he hadn't been preparing for Pro Day but his facial expression, and his attitude was so serious as if he knew this was the moment he had been waiting for.

When the time came to run the forty-yard dash he took his shirt off revealing a jello-like beer belly and ran a time slower than most of the linemen there. As if that wasn't embarrassing enough, he also did horribly in the field drills and often times provided comedic relief to everyone there. At the time, I too laughed at him, but now years later I wish he would have never shown up because out of all the memories I have of him, this one embarrassing moment is what I think of first when I hear his name. He, like many others, hoped he would do well but never prepared for it.

James Stockdale once said, "You must never confuse faith that you will prevail in the end, which you can never afford to lose, with the discipline to confront the most brutal facts of your current reality: and deal with it." Most of my Spartan brothers did the opposite of what Mr. Stockdale advised. Instead of facing the reality of the situation they were in and coming up with a process to better prepare themselves for their kairos moments, they allowed faith and hope to blur the truth about themselves and what would certainly happen as a result of not preparing.

I mentioned earlier that my father had some serious skills on the basketball court. That may actually be an understatement. Turns out the guy was really good. When I was little my dad used to play basketball at this place called Paul I Phillips in Grand Rapids Michigan. The city usually hosts this basketball tournament called "The Gus Mackers" and he was always one of the few key players people would want to see. One of the workers at Paul I told my dad that he had caught the recognition of an NBA recruiter and they were scouting him out. They set a date and time for him to try out for the league. My dad knew it but never made it to the gym.

I asked my mom where he was, and she responded, "Out in the street." She continued to tell me how she was too embarrassed to go down to the gym for the workout because she knew he wasn't there. "I just stayed home while they called asking where he was. I hate that he didn't take this opportunity because he was an excellent player," she told me.

I don't know when my father began smoking, but I do know it came about as a result of the people he grew up and hung around with. Now that doesn't relieve him of all accountability because at the end of the day we are all responsible for our own actions; nevertheless, the company he kept had an influence on him. My father would later be introduced to cocaine by his dad, and that would go on to solidify him as a career drug addict and convicted felon even to this day.

From time to time I think of my father and I wonder what if? What if this man, who had so much potential, would have only distanced himself from the bad influences of his friends and family? What if he would have made it to that workout and signed a contract with the NBA? What would our lives have looked like? What if he would have known the struggles and hardships we would go through if he continued down this road? How much pain could have been avoided? I may never know.

Through my father's failures, and my own, I've learned that not everyone around you has your best interest at heart, family included. And that doesn't necessarily make them bad people, although it could. It may very well be the plans they have for themselves, and what they want to do in life, doesn't coincide with the plans you have and what you want to do in life. We must always be mindful of the people we hang around because if we aren't, they can distract us from goals we have. I know that my father was used to spending hours on the basketball court perfecting his craft.

It's amazing how what took him multiple years to perfect, was destroyed in only a fraction of the time. All because of seeds planted by others. Check the company you keep and ask yourself, does this person really have your best interest at heart? Are they the type of people who will hold you accountable? Are they the type of people who will encourage you when you are down? Are they the type of people who will genuinely rejoice when

you rejoice or cry when you cry, or lend an ear
when you need to vent? Or are they the type of
people who will not only allow you to lose your
focus but are the cause of you losing your focus?
These are questions you will have to answer for
yourself. My hope is that you will be able to
objectively make the right decision.

Distractions can come in various forms such as a person or as a situation, examine your life and write down any potential distraction that can keep you from reaching your goal. Try to come up with a plan for overcoming these distractions.

_____

_____

_____

_____

_____

_____

_____

_____

_____

_____

_____

_____

_____

_____

_____

# Dan Orlovsky

There come multiple points, not one, but multiple, in our lives where people will tell you your dreams are too big. That your dreams are unrealistic, or that you should think of something, less your expectations or you aren't good enough. I want to encourage you that all you need is ONE person to believe in you; and that ONE person is YOU. Believe in yourself, believe in your dreams and aspirations. Believe in your character and your work ethic, and most importantly believe that your dreams can be your reality, no matter what anyone says. They're your dreams, not theirs.

# Dominic Raiola

Leave ... Your ... Mark

I was always told that I was too small, you're not big enough, you're not fast enough, you don't have what it takes ... You're from an island in the middle of the Pacific Ocean (Hawaii), they'll never hear about you ... To be the very best, sweat is necessary. You have to work when they sleep, be first, believe in yourself. For what you believe and want, no one can take away ... They can't replace your heart or your mind ... Why wouldn't you fight for what you want? Leave ... Your ... Mark.

Ecclesiastes 8:9

## Autistic Focus

Throughout the NFL every team has a series of meetings the night before kickoff to go over the game plan one last time. One night before our special team's meeting, the special team's coach, Joe Marciano, comes to me and shows me an exchange of text messages between him and his son, Joseph. Towards the end of the text thread, Joe tells his son, "Okay buddy it's almost 9:30. Shut your phone off. Go to bed. Talk to you tomorrow, sir." Joseph responded by saying, "I think you meant 9:30 PM, sir. You made a mistake, sir." Joseph has autism.

For those who do not know, autism is a complex developmental disorder that some people are born with. It typically affects a person's ability to communicate and form relationships amongst other things. Even though many look at those in Joseph's situation with great empathy, as they should, I believe we can also learn a great deal from our friends in the autistic community.

Tucked between the lines of what Joseph was saying to his father is one of the utmost principles missed by most people, that the little details are important. Because of his condition, Joseph can't help but focus on every detail. He sees them rather he wants to or not. Having an agonizing focus on the details is crucial to success no matter what profession or goal you have. Think of the doctor who is performing open heart surgery. He can't afford to move about casually. He has to have a laser-type focus. The level of detail he has to operate in literally is a matter of life and death for his patient. Or think of the symphony orchestra. Every musician has to be locked into the details of when their part starts and what notes to play for so many individuals to come together and form a beautiful sound. Or think of the detective who is examining a crime scene. He has to scan the area meticulously for every single detail to give him the best chance of solving his case.

There is no such thing as a little detail; this is also true in football. The average NFL play lasts three seconds, and the average special team's play can last anywhere from five to ten seconds. In that short amount of time, we players have to make various communications and adjustments while moving as humanly fast as possible. To do this, we have to be locked into every single detail before the play even starts. We must first assess the particulars of the situation as they will dictate the details of how we play when the ball is snapped. As I am running on the field before we punt, kick the ball to the opposing team, I'm looking at who's coming onto the field. I do this because from film study, I know how each player plays and how they will most likely try to cover me. Next, I'm looking at the opposing team's formation. Every team has a set of plays they run, some try to dress the plays up by moving guys around and every now and again teams give you new looks, but typically you can tell what a team is trying to do by the formation they align in. Next, I'm looking at our position on the field because I know our punter likes to punt a certain way depending on where he is aligned on the field. Furthermore, the down and distance give an indicator of if the opposing team plans to rush or play for a return. I gather all this information before the play even starts, and it puts me in the perfect position to have a plan of action once the ball is snapped. Now I'm ready to communicate with my teammates and alert them to any adjustments that may need to be made.

The job, however, is not yet done. The way I cover a punt depends on how the opponent covers me. More times than not, I will be double teamed,

and what is called a vice, this means that two
players will align side by side right in front of me
with the intentions of keeping me away from the
ball carrier. The only way for me to get down this
field and make a play is for me to have a tunnel-
like vision focus on the details. I know that I have
to get around one of these guys before they have a
chance to both grab me. This means my stance has
to be a certain way. My first step has to go a
certain way. I have to use my hands a certain way.
My eyes have to be looking at the right thing. And
I have to be the first aggressor because if I don't,
I'm putting myself in an even worse position than I
began in. When I do this the right way, I can beat
these two players, who often are faster, more
athletic, and younger than myself. Conversely,
when I do not, those five to ten seconds can feel
more like five to ten minutes because playing
gunner in the NFL, in my opinion, is the second
most brutal play, in football. The only thing that
surpasses being doubled as a gunner would be
playing offensive line on a field goal/ PAT.
Furthermore, I have to know the tendencies of the
returner. Is he a risk taker? Does he run side line to
side line or is he a downhill runner? Is he a
bulldozer or a shifty guy? All these factors come
into play as I prepare to attack him. If not done

rightly these two men will embarrass me or the returner will make me miss. But if done rightly, I will embarrass them and make a great play! Not because I'm better than they are. Remember at this stage of my career the players who align opposite of me are younger than I, faster than I, and more talented. I win because firstly I believe this play means more to me than it does the guys I'm going against. Secondly, I believe my focus exceeds their focus. I have trained myself to be able to focus autistically on the smallest detail during the heat of battle and this gives me the upper hand even though my body may not.

The perfect example of this came in our game against the Chicago Bears on October 18, 2015. We controlled the scoreboard most of the game and held a 24-16 lead going into the fourth quarter. However, the Bears were able to go on a run and score 15 points early in the fourth leading 31-24. We were able to fight our way back and force the game to go into overtime. We received the ball first but were not able to drive down for a score and found ourselves with a 4th & 10 situations pinned deep in our territory at the 18 yard line.

For those who don't know the overtime rules in the NFL, if the team who receives the ball first doesn't score a touchdown, the second team only needs to score a field goal to either win or continue the game. And since we hadn't scored at all, Chicago would only need a field goal to seal the deal. That makes this next play (punt) extremely crucial to us winning the game because the Bears had a strong footed kicker in veteran Robbie Gould who could easily bang a fifty-yard field goal through the uprights.

As I ran onto the field, I was gathering my usual data to prepare myself for the play ahead. There was a slight difference this time, though. Before we ran onto the field I told Sam Martin, Detroit Lion's punter, no matter what the situation was he was punting the ball to my side. So, there was the added pressure of that plus I have everyone looking at me to make a play, but in all honesty that didn't bother me one bit. The two guys who lined up against me were Sherrick McManis and Chris Prosinski. And the return man was Marc Mariani.

I mention these three by name because even though they may not be widely known household names, they are among the best special team players in the NFL and I have the utmost respect for them. Sherrick has solidified himself as one of the top cover men in the NFL as well as become a shutdown jammer. Over the years he and I have had some great battles. I was with Chris when he was drafted by the Jacksonville Jaguars. He is one of the most gifted players I've seen in a while and now has developed a savviness to go along with his God-given talent. Lastly, Marc is a former pro bowl return man who has a knack for finding the smallest crease and making a big play.

Needless to say, I am in a tough situation as I have two of the best special team guys in the NFL in front of me and another beast 50 yards deep waiting to return this punt. And depending on how well Sam punts the ball, they may only need a ten or fifteen yard return for a shot at a field goal. I know the only chance I have at making a play is to execute my technique flawlessly. So I take a deep breath and get in the proper stance then the ball is snapped. My first step is perfect. My eyes are looking at the perfect spot. My hand placement on Sherrick is perfect, which allowed me to grab and pull myself around him, thus turning a double team into a one on one. I know that there is no way I'm going to outrun Chris as he is super-fast. He ran 4.39 seconds in the forty-yard dash. And I can't let him get his hands on me or it's game over. I have to figure out a way to stop his feet so I can get by him. So, I fake an inside move, and he bites! I have him beat now.

Bringing down Marc in the open field is my next challenge. I knew from film study that he is a downhill guy, meaning he catches the ball and runs straight. So, I flashed in front of him to cause his feet to stutter, and that gave me the necessary time I needed to close in for the tackle for no gain. Sam booted the ball 60 yards in the air. And during that period I was able to get the best of three of the NFL's best players again, not because I'm better than they are, but because my focus at that moment exceeded their own.

The ability to slow the game down and focus on the right details may be innate to some people, but it was not a skill I was born with. I had to put a conscious effort into studying the most minute nuances of my position, as well as, glean insight from watching the best. Once I got an idea of how I wanted to build my game, I structured a practice routine in which I would mentally place myself in a game that moved at a snail's pace. In my mind, I would work on my stance, my eyes, my footwork, and my hand placement over and over again in my head.

Then when it came time for practice, I would start to implement my routine at a faster pace, with the emphasis being placed on doing the proper techniques rather than doing it fast and winning in that moment. Furthermore, I designed a workout routine that was geared toward strengthening the necessary parts of my body that I would need to become the best gunner in the NFL. Playing gunner can quickly become a nasty business, so I have to be able to strike and throw guys off of me fairly quickly. To be able to do this requires a strong grip, so I work on some various grip exercise every Wednesday and Thursday after practice. This is extremely helpful because as the season goes on, our bodies naturally begin to wear down; but, this routine helps to keep me strong and counter that effect. So, when others are getting weaker, my strength is constantly growing, which, in turn, gives me the upper hand.

I encourage you to do as I did. Sit down and write a full list of the ins and outs of what you will need to do to rise to the top of whatever career field you are seeking. Then come up with a routine that allows you to focus autistically on the necessary steps to get there. Become enamored with these details and so much so that even the slightest deviation sets off an alarm. I am a firm believer that we all can take a page from our friends in the autistic community in this regard.

One of my favorite movies is "Temple Grandin," which is based on a true story. In it an autistic girl named Mary Temple Grandin goes to stay with her aunt, who lives on a cattle ranch, and discovers her passion for cattle as well as her industrious ability to fix and design things. Temple becomes so enamored with providing cattle with a decent life before being killed for food that she became a leading activist for the humane treatment of livestock for slaughter.

She once said, "I think using animals for food is an ethical thing to do, but we've got to do it right. We've got to give those animals a decent life, and we've got to give them a painless death. We owe the animals respect." The fair treatment of animals meant so much to Temple that she placed herself in the animal's shoes, so to speak, and crawled through the process of leading an animal to slaughter so that she could see firsthand what the animals were experiencing.

She focused heavily on the smallest details so that she could ensure that the process would be as fast and as comfortable for the animal as humanly possible. As a result, Temple came up with a process that not only accomplished her goal of giving the animals a decent life and painless death; it also saved the companies money because animals no longer died prematurely during the process of becoming food.

Temple's commitment and focus on the most minute details is an example to us of how to do it rightly. Even though she dealt with the many struggles of autism and being neglected by society, Temple was able to block all of that out and lock into something she was truly passionate about. And her diligence yielded a great reward! Or take my case. I'm nowhere near the athlete that I used to be, but I can succeed in a line of work where the young and the strong dominate. Let our commitment be a reminder to you that no matter how hard things are and no matter how bad the hand life has dealt you, you can overcome it.

But it will take an extreme amount of focus over a long period. And you may not see the fruit of your labor for years and years ahead. But if you stay diligent and focus autistically on the task ahead and keep your head down and grind, I believe that by the time you look up, you'll be surprised at how successful you will have become.

The most successful people are those who focus autistically on the smallest details. Take a few moments and hone in on the most minute details of your goal. Write these details down and figure out a way to implement these details in your life on a daily basis. Remember it takes ninety consistent days of action before a new habit is formed.

_____

_____

_____

_____

_____

_____

_____

_____

_____

_____

_____

_____

# Josh Bynes

Work, Denial, Persevere, & Work some more!

When I was twelve years old, my Pop Warner football coach said, "You would never play high school ball or go to college and play ball!" As a kid to hear such a thing, almost crushes your hopes, dreams, and your spirits. I remember being so upset that I wanted to quit the team and not play football anymore. Instead, I stayed on the team and tried to work twenty times harder. I remember my Freshman year in college, football being so hard, that I called my mom and wanted to come home! My college coach told me I wouldn't make it in the NFL unless I played like another linebacker on the team. Instead, I stayed and worked harder than ever before.

Here I am, my sixth year in the NFL. The point is that people will deny you from the time you are "too small to play with the big kids." When your older siblings can do things you're not old enough to do yet. In life, there will be people who would doubt your ability and knowledge to do things you know you're capable of. It's not a time to run and hide! That's the time you work when no one is watching. Maybe even shed a tear or two. Through it all, persevere through adversity to become the person that you are destined to be. It could be a writer, a college professor, an inventor, you name it. Whatever you strive to be, never accept what people say about you. Just work, you will be denied at times, but you WILL persevere, and above all else, keep working!

# Maurice Williams

Never lose sight of the importance of being yourselves. Trying to be like someone else is hard, and rarely works out the way we desire it to happen. I believe that as much as we have in common with others, God has a unique purpose that he placed on the inside of each of us from the moment we were born. Take time to discover what you are good at, and what you are passionate about. The world is longing for your story, your gifting, and for your purpose to be fulfilled. What's on the inside of you has great value. Dare to be different and let your story impact the world for good.

## Branding Your Company

Before leaving the Lions in 2015, our special team's coach John Bonamego would always tell stories to prove a point. One of my favorites goes like this:

"There was an experiment done with five monkeys in a room. In the center of the room was a ladder with a banana tied to a string at the top. One monkey decides to go up the ladder and eat the banana. As soon as the monkey grabs the banana scalding hot water showers down on the other monkeys. The one on the ladder, however, wasn't harmed at all. The very next day a new banana is placed on the ladder and the same monkey goes up there. As soon as he grabs the banana again scalding hot water falls on the other monkeys.

This action goes on for a few days until the fifth day when one of the monkeys put two and two together and started to realize what was going on. He then began to spread the word to the rest of the group. Now everyone was waiting for that monkey to climb his monkey butt up there one more time. Sure enough, he starts up the ladder but before he could get halfway up the other four monkeys jump on him and beat the breaks off him. A day goes by and the same thing happens. Now several days have passed, and no one climbs the ladder anymore. The scientists decide to take one monkey out and replace him with a gorilla. The gorilla sees the banana at the top of the ladder and starts to climb but before he could get halfway up the other monkeys jump on him pretty bad.

Each day one monkey is replaced by a gorilla and that new gorilla tries to go up the ladder only to be met with the same beat down as the one before. The scientists continue to swap a monkey for a gorilla until all of the original animals were gone. The scientists were amazed to see that even though the gorillas never experienced the scalding hot water, they never went up the ladder and those who would dare to climb would be met with intense aggression by the rest of the group."

Firstly, this is not a real story, so please don't think I'm advocating for animal cruelty. Even though the story is comical, it has a very serious point behind it. Which is the importance of setting the right culture. The actions of the monkey in the first group put the rest of the guys at risk. Rather he knew it or not, his selfish ambition was the cause of everyone else's suffering. And that pain continued until the one monkey decided it was enough. I'm pretty sure that all of the monkeys were fed up with the situation and I imagine they would watch him and murmur amongst themselves. But it wasn't until one brave soul stood up and united the rest of the group behind him that real change began to happen.

Once everyone bought into the culture that was being set no one and nothing could come in and mess it up without a fight. Furthermore, when people, who never even knew the first struggle joined the team, they would come into an infrastructure that is so engrained in the atmosphere that it screamed this is how we do things here and if you want to be here you have to do it our way or the highway!

My first year at Norfolk State was very similar to the original five monkeys in the experiment. Many of us played the role of the first monkey who climbed the ladder by doing our own thing and seeking out our selfish ambitions regardless of if they hurt the team or not. Others would often murmur about what or who the problem was, but no one ever addressed it in front of the team. As a result, we won four games in 2005 and 2006. It wouldn't be until my junior year that we decided enough was enough. I would love to tell you that I was the one who rallied the troops and gave an amazingly unifying speech but that would be a lie.

Every captain made a collective effort to set a standard for the offense, defense, and special teams to follow and everyone bought into the culture we wanted to set. With the right culture in mind, we went from winning eight games in two years to winning eight games in 2007. We would then go on to lose the MEAC conference championship game to Delaware State University.

But the foundation of having a winning culture had finally been put into place. Norfolk State would go on to win the MEAC championship several years later, even though the players on the team didn't experience the struggles we had when I was there. They were able to benefit from the culture we set up and take it to a new level.

Having the right culture, the right environment, the right atmosphere around you is crucial to establishing your brand. Former Costco CEO Jim Sinegal once said, "Culture is not the most important thing, it is the only thing." He understood that if the culture wasn't right, then the brand would not be right. And if the brand was not right, the company would never reach its full potential. When you think of a brand what is the first thing that pops into your mind? Is it a particular shoe, Jordans? Or maybe a drink, Sprite? Or a company, Apple? A brand by definition is a marketing tool; rather it is a name, logo, slogan, or symbol, that is used to distinguish one business from the other, or one person from the other.

Imagine that you are the CEO of your company. And your job is to make sure that your company's brand, the marketing tool, is one that when customers see or hear about your company that they have nothing but positive things to say about it. What steps would you take to ensure that your brand is perceived the way you want it to be? How would you adjust the way you do business on a daily basis? What type of people would you hire to ensure a positive customer service experience?

Here is a little-known fact. You are the CEO of a company, and that company is you! Your brand, the marketing tool, is your abilities. The company you want to work for or the school you want to attend is the customer. You have to decide what the customer will think when they see or hear about your brand. Will your brand be more like a 7-Eleven or a Starbucks?

When you walk into a Starbucks, you know what you're going to get. You know there is going to be free wifi. You know that you will be greeted with a pleasant hello from the person working the register and that they are going to ask for your name. You know that when you place your order for a Caffè Latte, regardless of where you are, you will get the same drink, prepared the same, and with the same ingredients. You know that when your order is ready, they will call you personally by name. There is a level of consistency at Starbucks that reassures the customer of what their brand is every time they walk into a store.

Contrast that to 7-Eleven. You never know what you're going to get. When you walk in you may get a hello from the attendant at the register, or you may get a mean mug. If you go and get a cup of coffee from the coffee station, it may be hot or it may not. You may get excellent customer service, or you may hear the employees complaining about each other. It's possible that you may walk into a 7-Eleven and it will be the best 7-Eleven on the planet. But it's also possible to walk in there and be utterly disgusted by the appearance and employees. You just don't know. The consistency and assurance that you find at a Starbucks may or may not be found at 7-Eleven. And from a customer (employer) standpoint, they are looking for a consistent brand. They are looking for someone that they know they can rely on.

When people look at you what brand do they see? If there was a way for them to leave you a review, what rating would you get? This is not a rhetorical question nor should you try to personally answer this question because no matter how hard you try not to be, you are biased. Instead find several people who can be trusted to be brutally honest with you and ask them. Once you have their answers, then you can compare them to what you think about yourself. But remember, their perception, in this case, is the reality. If enough people believe you are a lazy person, there may be some truth there. The same can be said about someone who is hard working. Do not brush these opinions aside as in this case the customer is always right.

When a person sees that your brand is one that is consistent, trustworthy, reliable, and dependable, you will be amazed at how things begin to work out in your favor. There is an old proverb that says, "A good name is to be desired above great wealth." As an NFL player, I have seen and personally experienced having great wealth one minute and seeing it seemingly disappear the next. Finances, like all material things, are extremely finite and temporal. But a good name and a trustworthy brand can go a long way in helping you throughout life. People, generally speaking are wired to trust what others say about a person.

If your brand has an excellent report with others, it can actually act similar to like a line of credit for later endeavors. Based on what you've previously done, people will give the benefit of the doubt and support what you have going on or even support something simply because your involved with it. The perfect example of this is Hollywood. Think of your favorite movie actor(s). My favorite actors are Will Smith, Denzel Washington, and Leonardo DiCaprio. These men have built a brand so strong that people, myself included, will pay money to see a movie just because they are in it. Or think of a famous place like Disney World. They have branded themselves as the "place where dreams come true," and over the years have lived up to that brand, so much so that people call it the happiest place on Earth.

From the moment you arrive there, every attendant, Disney character, cashier, janitor, and security guard are all working hard to make sure you experience that magical feeling they've grown to be known for. As a result, they can charge higher prices and people are willing to pay because they know what they are going to get.

## How Do You Establish Your Brand?

How do you make sure that the person you think you are is actually the person that people see? This will require some research on your part. I suggest that you find four or five individuals who are doing or have done, what you want to do and who exemplify the characteristics you want people to see or think of when they see you and do your best to imitate them. Aristotle once said, "What is valuable and pleasant to a morally good man actually is valuable and pleasant." In other words, if you want to know how to live rightly, model yourself after someone who is living rightly.

I think one of the greatest hindrances to the next generation fulfilling their goals is their ignorance to the efforts and strategies of previous generations. A perfect example of this is the "Black Lives Matter Organization." In the midst of heavy racial tensions throughout America, three African American women came on the scene with a brilliant slogan that "Black Lives Matter." This slogan quickly became a national movement as many Americans, both within the African American community and outside it, felt as if there is some effort to oppress or demean the value of the black life.

The magnificence of this organization is also its "Achilles Heel." At its core, the Black Lives Matter organization lacks leadership. Meaning there is no one, no CEO, to steer the movement and control the brand that people see. Instead, they have different factions doing their own thing, often acting on impulsive rage rather than logic &

strategy. As a result, the way people see and think of this organization is drastically different depending on where you are in the country. This, in most cases, is a result of the organization's brand being perceived drastically different throughout the country. It, in essence is 7-Eleven.

Let's contrast the rise of the Black Lives Matter movement to the rise of the Civil Rights movement. In the midst of racial tension in the 1950s, African Americans began to boycott the Montgomery, Alabama bus system, led by a young preacher named Martin L. King, in protest against segregated seating. Today this movement is known as the Montgomery Bus boycott. This movement began just days after an African American woman, Rosa Parks, refused to give up her seat on a bus for a white man. The boycott lasted a little more than a year and is touted as the first large-scale demonstration against segregation in American history.

Because of Rosa's bravery and because of the success of the boycott, the Supreme Court ordered the city of Montgomery to integrate its bus system. The interesting fact to point out here is that Rosa Parks was not the first person to refuse to give up her seat. Several months earlier a 15-year-old African American girl refused to give up her seat to a white woman. As a result, she was arrested. Leaders like Dr. King didn't want to use Claudette's case as the face of the movement because she was pregnant by a married man and had a history of being a problem child.

Civil rights leaders waited for a Rosa Parks to come along before they launched their movement. They understood the importance of branding concerning getting their mission accomplished. Rather you agreed with Dr. King and his efforts or not, one thing you couldn't mistake was his brand. You knew what you were going to get when you saw him. You knew his protests were going to be peaceful; you knew he was going to give a passionate speech to ignite the people. You knew he was going to be strategic in his movements, even though some tried to paint Dr. King as public enemy number one. His brand was so well established that they couldn't tarnish his image.

One of the differences between the founders of the Black Lives Matter organization and Dr. King is the amount of emphasis placed on branding. So far, we've seen that the Black Lives Matter organization doesn't put that much stock into it whereas Dr. King, as well as other Civil Rights leaders, did. They knew that the only way to get their mission accomplished was to get America on their side and establishing the right brand set the foundation for what would come after.

I believe that the Black Lives Matter organization is seeking a noble cause. But no matter how noble a cause it may be, if it is not portrayed correctly it runs the risk of being ineffective in the long run. I believe the Black Lives Matter organization would be far more impactful if it would adopt the same strategic approach to civil rights as our predecessors as they have given us the road map to making effective change and there is no reason to try and re-invent the wheel.

I've said all this not to demean or attack the Black Lives Matter organization; I only want to point out how important establishing the right brand is. You may have a dream or a goal or something that you may want to accomplish. That goal may even be revolutionary and life-changing. But if it is not branded correctly, and if you as the CEO does not steer it in the right direction, you open the door for naysayers to kill your dream before it takes off. Learn from those who have come before you. Implement their successes and avoid their mistakes. There are very few things we can control in life. Accurately establishing the right brand is not one of them.

Your brand is the impression that others walk away with when they come into contact with you. List the characteristics that you want to be known for. What are steps you can take to make these characteristics a part of who you are?

_____

_____

_____

_____

_____

_____

_____

_____

_____

_____

_____

_____

_____

_____

# Glover Quin

If you don't know where you're going, how will you know when you get there!

When I talk to people, I always use the analogy of a someone driving a car using a GPS to get to their destination! Once you put that destination into the GPS, you will be directed to get there! It may take you to a path that you were not expecting! You may miss a turn, and it will redirect you! You may stop and get gas, but once you get back in the car, it will instruct you to keep going toward the destination! There may be traffic, obstacles, even hazards in the road that you may have to go through to get to your destination! Picture life the same way! Have a goal or destination in mind! On your journey, you will go through various obstacles, make many mistakes, question if this is even the journey you want to be on! As long as you have that destination, you will be redirected through the traffic, from the wrong turn, and around the hazard to get there! Always have a destination that you are trying to get to! When you are trying to get to the top or wherever you are trying to go, you won't settle for stopping short of the destination!

# Rashad Jennings

Throughout my incredible journey, I've learned that you can pretty much count on the fact that each day you get to practice being the person you will become. If you waste time each day, then you are practicing to waste your life and deprive the world of the greatness that might have been. If you work hard at noble things that not only benefit you but others, then you are practicing to become a great blessing to the world.

Someone smarter than myself said these things: Every day you get the same 24 hours that everyone else gets. What you do with that time is up to you. Aim at nothing, and you are almost guaranteed to hit it every single time. Shoot for the moon, and even if you miss, you will be among the stars. Those words might sound cliche', but I am a living witness that they are absolutely true!

Finally, it is absolutely impossible to look into the eyes of a human being and imagine he or she is the product of anything else but an awesome God. Always look in the mirror and remind yourself that you were created for greatness!

## The Me, Myself, & I Fallacy

During my senior year at Norfolk State, I remember an NFL scout coming by to meet with me. As we went into the film room, he asked our wide receiver coach if I was a good player. The coach responded, "yeah, he is definitely self-made". I loved hearing that because after all the pain I had been through in my childhood, I decided to lump everything that ever hurt me into a box and from that moment on if I wanted something I was going to get it myself. And I kept that same mindset all throughout my youth and college years. It wasn't until my second year in the NFL that I realized the me, myself, and I mindset that I had was not only a fallacy, which is a false belief but also was a slap in the face of all the people who helped mold me into the man I am today.

Like any other professional athlete, I am often asked: "What professional player(s) did I look up to as a child?" And I enjoy watching their faces when I tell them none. Before high school, I couldn't tell you who played for what NFL team and could barely even tell who the teams themselves were. I started playing football simply because I wanted to hang out with my older cousins and because of the age gap, football was basically the only common denominator between us, apart from being related of course.

Most of the time they would designate me the all-time snapper and give me the name of some player to make me feel good as we played in the front yards or basement of our grandfather's church. I couldn't care less who the player was, I was just glad to be with them.

The more we played together, the more I realized the only chance I had of actually catching a ball instead of snapping it was to get better. So I began to try and imitate the way they played. I modeled my game after everything they did and even though they never really noticed my improvements, it was clear to see that when I went up against kids in my neighborhood that most of the time I was a little better.

Not because I was naturally more gifted than them, but because I had been refining my skills against guys who were bigger, faster, and stronger than I. If my cousins didn't play football, I doubt I would have played. Even though I am the one who made it to the NFL, it would not have been possible without their influences in my life. The passion that I have for this great game came from my eagerness to hang with my cousins. I didn't develop this on my own.

## More Than I Bargained For

I was once told that if I wanted to be successful, all I would need to do is find someone who is doing what I want to do and model myself after that person. I have found this to be a true statement, but there is a caveat. Not everyone who is doing what you want to do in life should be used as a good example for you. This was never more real a statement for me then it was my rookie year in the NFL. After injuring my shoulder early in the Cleveland Browns training camp, I was sent down to the Jacksonville Jaguars. As I walked into the locker room, I saw a guy who I grew up watching since my days in high school.

With great excitement, I went up to him to introduce myself and ask him for coaching points on making it to where he was. His response, however, left me speechless and slightly embarrassed. He looked me in the face and said, "Yeah I'll coach you up, I'll coach you right to the bench. This is a competition." After I had picked my jaw up off the ground, I laughed off his statement and went on my way. I learned a very important lesson that day. Even though this was a great and successful player, he was not the right person for me to follow.

Now let's contrast that experience to the first time I met Rashean Mathis. I've already stated in chapter three that no other NFL player has had a greater impact on me than he has. But that influence extended well beyond the game of football as well. I am always happy to tell people how Rashean helped me to become a professional football player. But I'm more excited to share how he helped me become a man. And not just any man, but a man of God. Before I met Rashean and several other players I was the typical hot-headed rookie looking to have a good time and live that baller life that is portrayed on television.

With my shoulder injury, I didn't play my first year which left me with a whole lot of time on my hands and a bunch of money burning a hole in my pockets. I would come into the facility and brag about the sexual escapades and thrilling nights I was having while on Miami's South Beach.

Rashean would be that constant moral voice in my ear, never judging me, but lovingly correcting and trying to steer me in the right direction. It took a little more than a year before I started to realize that the life I was living was one of selfishness and destruction. It was at that time that Rashean, and others, stepped in and showed me a better way to live. A life that is full of love, joy, peace, and a sound mind. They not only cared about Don Carey, the player, but they also cared about Don Carey, the person as well.

And so much so that they spent countless hours of prayer, Bible study, and genuine brotherhood to help solidify me in my faith. Yes, it is true that you can learn how to be successful from watching other successful people in your desired field. But try, if you can, to find someone who will not only impact your career for the better but your life as well.

## Some Things Only Come With Age

Several years ago my wife and I began to ramp up the activity in our property management company. Up until that point, we had only acquired a few properties and really hadn't done much with them. One day after practice in 2014, Coach Caldwell came to me and inquired about our business model regarding property acquisition and management. I proudly spat out our business plan and what I wanted to do moving forward.

Coach smiled and told me I was going about it the wrong way. Even though there wasn't anything wrong with what I was doing, Coach wanted to give me a much better way of doing business. Throughout the years, he has run a very successful property management. He spent nearly an hour with me on a dry erase board going over all the details of his real estate business strategy, taking the time to make sure I understood every detail of how to go about my business. Since then I've worked on nearly twenty properties buying, selling, building and managing them.

Coach Caldwell has been one of the best mentors I have ever had. He truly has an uncanny ability to lead and inspire as well as the wisdom and experience to place you in the most optimal position to succeed. I've never met a man, player or coach, who wouldn't run through a brick wall for him. I hope and pray that if I am blessed to reach his age, that I too am able to lead, inspire and encourage others like he has done for countless people.

Because of his willingness to teach me, my wife and I are now well on our way to establishing a legacy to pass down to our children and a company that will change the lives of so many people. But none of that would have been possible had I kept that same me, myself and I mindset because I was so focused on doing things my way, for myself, and by myself.

It is one thing to want to do something your own way. But never get so locked into one way of thinking that you can't heed the words of those who have come before you and have laid the footprint for success!

## The William Robinson Affect

The allure of being self-made was very appealing to me because it validated the "me, myself, and I" mindset that I took on when I was younger. But now that I am an adult looking back on my younger years, I would not have become the man I am today had it not been for the myriads of people who have sown into my life. Several of which I want to mention apart from my mother, none have been more influential than my stepdad William H. Robinson III.

From the very first moment I met my stepdad (Rob), he has been that continual male presence in my life that I had been longing for so many years. Rob is one of the types of men that if you saw him walking down the street, you may quickly misjudge this book by its cover. On the outside, Rob is a six-foot-three, two hundred and fifty-pound man with a unique facial expression that can only be found on someone from the northside of Pittsburgh, PA.

When someone tries to mimic my dad, they always add this snarling look on their face accompanied by a growling baritone voice. He truly fits the visual idea of what a manly man looks like, but that's just the outward appearance. Don't get me wrong, his attitude and persona back up his appearance but as the saying goes, "Still waters run deep." There is far more to this man than I first realized when I met him. Inside of his wrought iron shell exists a man full of compassion, wisdom, love, humility, and faithfulness. And throughout the years I have learned so many lessons from him, three of which I will share with you in the following paragraphs.

Shortly after our move to Norfolk, VA, I came home to the shock that my dresser had disappeared and my clothes were on the bed. I asked my parents what happened with it and Rob replied by telling me he wanted me to fold my clothes a certain way and he wanted me to place them in a particular spot in my room. Rob would then check to make sure I was keeping in line with his commands periodically.

This went on for nearly a year before they bought me a dresser again. I can't say that I fully understood what was going on at the time. Part of me felt as if I was in one of those movies were the parent treated their stepchild unfairly. But that couldn't be the case because Rob was one of the coolest dudes I ever met and he didn't treat me any different than he did his own son.

So, what would cause Rob to take my dresser? Well, Rob was a retired Navy veteran who served on the USS Eisenhower. And when he saw me he saw a young kid who lacked discipline. And his way of teaching it to me was to act militarily. You see in the military you have to do things a certain way. You have to wake up at a certain time, make your bed a certain way, talk a certain way, etc. All this is done with the purpose of instilling discipline into the troops. Even though Rob didn't run his house like a military general, it was evident that he spent some time there from the way he did things.

Initially, I absolutely hated not having a dresser and having to fold my clothes. But as the months went on I began to take pride in it and so much so that even to this day I fold and hang my clothes a certain way. The discipline I learned from Rob also affected other areas of my life as well. As an NFL veteran, I have a routine that I've been following for years now. And my ability to stick to it religiously stems from the lessons I learned when I was a fourteen-year-old kid.

Rob once asked me what I wanted to do in life and I told him my dream was to be an NFL player. I then had to write out a three-step plan to get there. Step one was to graduate high school because I couldn't make it to the NFL unless I went to college. Step two was to graduate college. Step three was to make it to the NFL. I wrote my goals on a note card and placed it on my headboard in my room.

Rob had me do this because he wanted my goals to be the last thing I saw at night and the first thing I saw when I woke up. This is crucial because every day you wake up and roll out of bed there are going to be people acting contrary to your goals. And with all the distractions that come along with friends, family, and foes, it's important that you have a daily reminder that you have a goal that you are trying to reach.

Some of the most gratifying moments of my life came when I checked off my goals. There is something encouraging about seeing yourself inch closer and closer to your dream, and every time I reached a new goal, it made me want to work even harder to achieve the next one. If you haven't already done so, I implore you to write out your goal. Then come up with a three-step plan to get there. The plan doesn't have to be super detailed, but it does need to be realistic, obtainable, and on a time scale. I suggest the short-term, mid-term, and long-term approach.

Let the short term be what you expect to accomplish within the next year or two. The midterm is what you plan to accomplish within five years. Finally, the long term represents the accomplishing of your goal within a decade. Here is the cool thing about this approach. Once you've reached your long-term goal, you can easily start the cycle all over again with a new set of goals and a new plan. Be sure to put your goals in a place where you can see them constantly so they can remind you of where you are trying to go and what you are trying to do in life.

Lastly, throughout the years I've seen Rob bend over backward to help others. I've seen him do everything from co-founding a non-profit organization called P.R.E.P.S. (Player Resources Education and Preparation Skills), which provides athletes and parents high school and NCAA eligibility requirements and entrance information with emphasis on Science, Technology, Engineering and Mathematics (STEM), to opening the doors of our home to family needing help to get back on their feet.

From his constant acts of selflessness, I've learned that real success is not only defined by the number of milestones we obtain for ourselves, but also by the number of people we reach back and pull along the way. It is easy to go about your day only focusing on yourself. There is nothing wrong with wanting to make sure you are taken care of. But as I said earlier in chapter four, none of us is born in a bubble. Nor will we grow up in one. It is vitally important that we push those around us to be just as successful as ourselves.

As human beings, we are designed for community and each person within every community has a vital role to play not only for the bettering of themselves but also for the bettering of his and her neighbor as well! One of my favorite quotes comes from one of the most infamously known men in human history. Adolf Hitler once said, "He alone who owns the youth gains the future." He understood the importance of sowing into the next generation in regards to getting a particular agenda accomplished.

Now I completely disagree with what Hitler wanted to do with the youth. Nevertheless, I think these words are so true! Our children are our future. If we have an impact on our children, especially at a young age, we will impact our future. Just as Rob has given so much to help the next generation, I hope this book will aid in my continual efforts to do the same. Additionally, I hope that as you obtain the success you are looking for, that you would also reach back and pull someone with you as well!

Just as Rob challenged me, I am now challenging you to write down a three step plan to reach your goal. Remember that your short term goal is something you plan to accomplish in one year. The mid-term goal is something you can accomplish in five years. The long term goal is something that can be accomplished in 10 years. Place this plan somewhere you can see it every single day.

_____

_____

_____

_____

_____

_____

_____

_____

_____

_____

_____

_____

## Final Thoughts

Writing this book has been one of the most humbling experiences I've ever had. I am truly honored that you have chosen to go on this journey of my life with me. Everything you have read up until this point has been written with the sole purpose of hopefully giving you the feeling that if Don Carey can achieve his goals, then so can you. I often tell people that my story is not unique yet it is very unique.

It is not unique because I, like many others, have experienced the hardship of being raised without a father by a mother who struggled to provide us with the best life possible. It is not unique because I, like most NFL players, look just like you. It is not unique because the same principles that I live by are the same principles that have helped countless numbers of people throughout the years and are the same principles that you can benefit from as well. It is, however, unique in the fact that it is my story with my details. Just as your story is unique to you with its own details.

Now that you have read everything, the next question you should ask is what does this mean to me? Sure, there may be a lot of great, inspiring information in this book, but you have to find a way to make this make sense in your life. Remember the stories are all principle based. And from each of them, you can pull some insight or nugget that can be applied to your life. There may also be parts of this book that don't apply to you. But that doesn't mean you throw the baby out with the bathwater. As I said before, pull from these pages whatever you need to help you do what you want to do in life at a higher level. So as this book comes to an end, I'd like to leave you with some final thoughts.

1. Don't be perfect, be coachable. Sure, there may come a time when you will be able to do something perfectly. But until you reach that point, make sure you are open to learning from the mistakes you make along the way. And make sure you remain humble and open to correction from others. Everyone wants perfection. You want it and so do I. But the reality is this; we are flawed beings and the likelihood of us reaching perfection will inevitably to stiffened due to us constantly making mistakes. But we can't allow that to slow

us down. Matthew Syed once said, "Failure to learn from mistakes has been one of the single greatest obstacles to human progress." Remaining coachable allows you to fix any problems along the road to success.

2. *"Dare to dream big"* Michelangelo once said, "The greatest danger for most of us is not that our aim is too high and we miss it, but that it's too low and we achieve it." I know that many of you reading this have grown up in situations similar to mine or maybe even worse. One of the reasons I've been able to escape the generational curse of drugs and violence that plagues my family tree is the fact I never stopped dreaming! My dream to change my situation and have a better life for my children than I had, was a constant reminder to me that I was going someplace.

Take a page out of Barrington Irvin's life. For those who don't know, he was an African American man who built and flew his own plane around the world at the age of 23. So many people doubted him and said he couldn't do it. But he had a dream and even though the people around him didn't see his vision, the fact that he could see it was more than enough. Dare to dream and dream big. Dare to be different. Dare to change your situation. Dare to change the world!

3. Never put off until tomorrow, what can be done today. The sooner you find out what you want to do in life. And the sooner you set in place a game plan to reach that goal. The better chance you have of actually getting there. Tomorrow is a luxury that none of us are promised. Therefore, there is no better time to prepare for your future than right now. Don't think that you have to wait until you are up in your years to accomplish your goals.

People who think this way often find themselves regretting the years they wasted. There is no such thing as being too young. While watching the Olympics this past year, I was amazed at the number of athletes who were under the age of 25. Here we have the best of the best in the world competing on one of the largest stages in the world, and the vast majority of the athletes were young adults.

4. Be mindful of the footprints you leave. It doesn't matter what you do in life there will always be someone watching you whether it be

your children or someone outside your home, with each step you take, always remember that you are leaving footprints that will inevitably be followed by someone. Rather you want them to follow you or not is irrelevant, that part you cannot control. You can, however, control where those footprints lead. And you will have to decide if your footprints will lead them down a path to success and right living or will your footprints lead them down a path of inevitable failure and mediocrity.

5. Finally, when you reach that point of success. Take time to reach back and pull someone else along the way. Don't be afraid to be open and transparent about the successes and failures because I can promise you that there is someone out there who needs to meet you, see your video, listen to your lecture, read your book, or hear your life story to gain the necessary inspiration for them to succeed.

Be Blessed!

## Author Bio

Don J. Carey III was raised in Hampton Roads, VA where he and his family still reside. In 2014 he and his wife Lakeisha married and had their first son Victor one year later. Don received his Bachelor's degree in Building Construction Technology from Norfolk State University and shortly after was drafted into the NFL. He has spent the last eight years in the league playing two years with the Jacksonville Jaguars and is currently in his 6th year with the Detroit Lions. He is currently studying to receive his Masters in Theological Studies with a focus in the Old Testament from Moody Theological Seminary.

Don is also the founder of DCIM; a para-church organization geared towards reaching, teaching, and releasing disciples for Christ. In 2012 Don and his wife Lakeisha started C&R Preferred, LLC which is a property management company based out of Virginia.

In 2016 Don was nominated for Walter Payton Man of the Year award, which will be given an NFL player for his outstanding commitment to community service. In the offseason, Don and his wife travel the country speaking and motivating the next generation to think critically and take advantage of every opportunity to better themselves.